THE SYSTEM
from Pure Potential to Enlightenment

THE SYSTEM
from Pure Potential to Enlightenment

Mark Ty-Wharton

mark.ty-wharton.com
All rights reserved © 2014

Copyright © 2014 by Mark Ty-Wharton

All rights reserved. This book or any portion thereof may not be reproduced or used in any manner whatsoever without the express written permission of the publisher except for the use of brief quotations in a book review or scholarly journal.

First Printing: 2014

ISBN 978-1-291-97239-9

THE SYSTEM
Mark Ty-Wharton
Glastonbury
Land of the Summer People
United Kingdom

THESYSTEM@mark.ty-wharton.com

Ordering Information:

BUY Cards from: http://thesystemcards.com
BUY Music from iTunes: https://itunes.apple.com/album/the-system/id909406190
LISTEN FREE: https://play.spotify.com/search/Mark Ty-Wharton/albums

Special discounts are available on quantity purchases of books, CDs and cards by corporations, associations, educators, and others. For details, contact the publisher at the above listed email address.

Dedication

To everlasting life, we are in this together.

Contents

Frequently Asked Questions ix
Preface xi
Introduction 1
A Harlequin's Journey 3
THE SYSTEM 5
I: POTENTIAL 9
II: IDENTITY 10
III: OPPORTUNITY 11
IV: INTUITION 12
V: FRIENDSHIP 13
VI: ADVENTURE 14
VII: CREATIVITY 15
VIII: RESPONSIBILITY 16
IX: INTELLECT 17
X: ACTION 18
XI: ALLIANCE 19
XII: TIME 21
XIII: CHOICE 22
XIV: GENEROSITY 23
XV: CHARACTER 24
XVI: MEANING 25
XVII: REFLECTION 26
XVIII: POWER 27

XIX: CHAOS 28
XX: TRUTH 30
XXI: FAIRNESS 31
XXII: CONTEXT 32
XXIII: FAITH 33
XXIV: GROWTH 34
XXV: CHANGES 35
XXVI: LAUGHTER 36
XXVII: BALANCE 37
XXVIII: SOUL 38
XXIX: TEARS 39
XXX: SHADOW 40
XXXI: METAMORPHOSIS 42
XXXII: RETREAT 43
XXXIII: REBIRTH 44
XXXIV: IMAGINATION 45
XXXV: HOPE 47
XXXVI: ANGER 48
XXXVII: APPROVAL 49
XXXVIII: PEACE 51
XXXIX: FREEDOM 52
XXXX: SUCCESS 53
Notes 54

Frequently Asked Questions

What is it? This book can be used alone, or as an accompaniment to a set of oracle cards and a concept album of the same name, which depicts a journey from pure potential to actualisation.

Who can use it? Anybody with an interest in actualisation, the seven chakras, the twelve constellations, or tarot.

How do I get started? If you want to get started straight away, you can simply open the book, pick a page and read the description.

Where can I buy the cards or the album? You can order the book, cards and CD online, or from select retailers. You can buy the eBook for your iPad or Kindle. You can buy the sound journey from over 200 digital outlets online including Amazon, Beatport, eMusic and iTunes Music Store. You can even listen to it on Spotify.

What is the difference between v1 and v2? Version 1 cards are like traditional trumps. They have even been designed so that you can play the game with them. Version 2 cards are more like a full size Tarot deck and include two additional potentials cards. Other than that the card names and THE SYSTEM itself remains the same.

Why is it called the system? All good card players have a system. Human beings are by default story tellers. We derive meaning and story from everything we do. Everything that happens in life follows a story. Be it a professional, personal or private conflict, each story has its own arc. In some realms of personal development it is said that who we really are is our story about ourselves. Pick any card in the deck, and it will relate to a place on an arc of one of the stories that you are in life. It works in exactly the same way as the Fools Journey in Tarot.

Is the system new? Yes and no. The system is based on existing systems such as the seven chakras, the twelve constellations and the Major Arcana, or trump cards in Tarot. THE SYSTEM is a new way of looking at something established and traditional.

Who invented it? You could say that life did. I am a Reiki Master/Teacher, and on my own spiritual journey I have encountered many systems. Clairvoyance, iChing, Self-realisation, Tai Chi, Tarot and various forms of Yoga. I am on the autistic spectrum and I recognise patterns. This puts me in a unique position of being able to understand systems and draw correlations between them.

Will I become actualised if I use this deck? All good path leads to enlightenment. Yet nobody becomes enlightened. You already are what you are, it is possible that has not been seen yet?

What are the key concepts used in cards? The "I", "me", or "self" is an "ego trick" which hides "innate truth." It can simply vanish and then what shows up is: Life – seen as a possibility for awareness, capacity for experience. Liberty.

Everything is always in flux. Nothing is ever fixed; even the relationships between things are in flux and ever changing. The idea that things are fixed or can be constant is only ever a concept.

Everything about reality simply changes, happens and moves. Everything that human beings create in order to try and make sense of the world we live in is made up. Even this book!

It will help to think of this book as a set of ideas which can bring a sense of clarity to chaos. This book is not intended to be an answer. It contains ideas about places to look which ultimately unveil your own answer.

Preface

THE SYSTEM was born out of three ideas. The first idea is from 1999 and came after I was presented with a small colourful inspirational card at a vocal workshop. The second came more recently: While trying to make sense of the order of the as yet still incomplete manuscript for my next book, I decided to create a set of cards which depict each the key concepts it talks about. The third is that life is a gamble and if we present life as a deck of cards, every good card player should have a system.

My original idea was to create a new trump set which paralleled the Major Arcana in medieval Tarot. I designed a deck as a guide for daily inspiration and used it for problem solving.

THE SYSTEM expands on the idea of problem solving, by recognising that life is full of professional, personal and private conflicts. Human beings are natural story tellers and each of those conflicts has its own story arc.

You can use Tarot to tell a story. The Major Arcana of Tarot follows a story arc. In the story we follow the journey of a Fool through each of twenty one doorways to completion.

To expand on the original idea, I included two other systems: The seven chakras and the twelve constellations.

The oracle deck is based on a harlequin's journey which takes the questioner on the mythological voyage of a hero, along a symbolic path to actualisation.

The interpretations encompass various teachings, while holding no affiliation to any single religion or organisation.

Mark Ty-Wharton

Introduction

If you have purchased the cards that go with this book, you can use the deck in a variety of ways, including any of the traditional Tarot spreads. You can follow the entire journey of the book by listening to the sound journey, or by reading the book from cover to cover chronologically. Alternatively, you can simply open the book at a random page, or pull a card from the deck to reflect the current mood of momentum.

I recommend the following spread.

The Three Card Spread
Method

Card 1: Is central to the reading and reflects your current situation or mood.
Card 2: Place this card to the left of Card 1. This card relates to memory patterns (both conscious and unconscious) which are affecting the current situation or mood.
Card 3: Place this card to the right of Card 1. This card relates to imagination and the perceived outcome of the current situation or mood based on circumstances and beliefs.

Interpretation
There is no fixed answer, a reading is more like a snapshot of a state of affairs and because any given state of affairs is always in flux, the flow of a reading can often alter in the light of new information.

We live in a world where everything is increasingly defined in terms of a yes/no response. The world clearly doesn't work in this way and solutions are often about putting things into balance.

Perhaps human beings do everything based on love or fear? Whether or not this is true, it is a useful illustration to help in understanding this method of interpretation.

THE SYSTEM

It is clear to most of us there are dramatically different degrees of love or fear. If a card does not appear to relate to you, try not to discard the card, but to work with it. Decide to what degree in your life the card you picked holds meaning for you.

How does it relate to your question/situation. How would working on this area effect the outcomes in your life. Nine times out of ten, your card will appear to relate directly to your problem anyway.

I'll let you into a secret. Language isn't absolute. There simply aren't enough words to describe all the variables. It is all an interpretation.

Finally, while thinking about the problem you can ask:

Who do you not forgive?
Who is it that is suffering?

What do you regret?
What is in the way of simply being?

When will you choose the answer?
When can you resolve it?

Where is there fear?
Where can "that which is hidden" be expressed?

Why do you think you are?

How would it be resolved if you weren't you?

A Harlequin's Journey

The four stages of the journey marked out by the oracle cards, album and book are as follows:

SEPARATION
(Ordinary World)

PILGRIMAGE
(First Threshold - Special World - The Seeker)

REVOLUTION
(Second Threshold - Battle - The Crusader)

ACTUALISATION
(Third Threshold - Suffering - The Return)

When the sage notices separation, they set out to complete themselves, only to discover that the "ego trick" of "I", "me", or "self" is an illusion.

A "true sage" must be willing to give up everything they believe in, to actualise "innate truth".

Only then can the rites of passage be complete and the sage re-enters society with true status.

THE SYSTEM

Mark Ty-Wharton

THE SYSTEM

ø ARC OF IDENTITY:
Follows a journey along an ancient symbolic esoteric path.
(the 21 doors)
µ CIRCLE OF ILLUSION:
Follows the mythological voyage of a hero.
(the twelve constellations)
¿ PATH OF THE CHILD:
Follows a journey to liberation.
(the seven keystones)
\# RITES OF PASSAGE:
A chronological journey to enlightenment.
± PHYSIOMOTIONAL:
Marks the thesis, antithesis and eventual synthesis of a dialectic that arrives at the truth by exchanging logical arguments.

THE FORMULA

SEPARATION
(Ordinary World)

µ *Lack of belonging*
~ POTENTIAL

µ *Life reveals a problem (something missing)*
µ IDENTITY
ø OPPORTUNITY

µ *It takes more than a sign to incite a reaction*
ø INTUITION
¿ FRIENDSHIP
µ ADVENTURE

THE SYSTEM

μ *See you on the other side of the looking glass*
ø CREATIVITY
ø RESPONSIBILITY
ø INTELLECT
μ ACTION

PILGRIMAGE
(First Threshold - Special World - The Seeker)

μ *The tip of the iceberg*
ø ALLIANCE
μ TIME
ø CHOICE
¿ GENEROSITY

μ *Unexpected aspects cause disorientation*
ø CHARACTER
μ MEANING
ø REFLECTION
¿ POWER

μ *A life or death situation (sometimes figurative)*
ø CHAOS
¿ TRUTH
ø FAIRNESS
μ CONTEXT

REVOLUTION
(Second Threshold - Battle - The Crusader)

μ *Do what thou wilt (use everything for growth)*
ø FAITH
μ GROWTH
ø CHANGES
¿ LAUGHTER

μ *The dark night of the soul*
ø BALANCE
μ SOUL
¿ TEARS
ø SHADOW

μ *Rising from the ashes*
μ METAMORPHOSIS
ø RETREAT
ø REBIRTH
ø IMAGINATION

ACTUALISATION
(Third Threshold - Suffering - The Return)

μ *Must be willing to give up everything for actualisation*
ø HOPE
μ ANGER
ø APPROVAL

μ *Master of two worlds (the battle won)*
¿ PEACE
μ FREEDOM
ø SUCCESS

THE SYSTEM

Mark Ty-Wharton

I: POTENTIAL

SEPARATION
(Ordinary World)

The illusion of separation orphans us from the truth of what we really are. A "true sage" begins a journey of contemplation full of hope, without concept of risk. In this momentum, carefree, full of curious wonder and infinite potential, as heroic as the uncarved block.

Innocence, discovery, moving forward into the unknown. Without a care for where the journey will end.

ARC OF IDENTITY	0
CIRCLE OF ILLUSION	1
PATH OF THE CHILD	0
RITES OF PASSAGE	1
EXPRESSION	0
PHYSIOMOTIONAL	~
COLOUR / SYMBOL	FOOL
KEYSTONES & MNEMONICS	I DON'T BELONG
ELEMENT/IDIOM	SPACE/NOTHING

THE SYSTEM

II: IDENTITY

You know what your trouble is?
You don't have the faintest idea what you are!
You have misidentified an emotion or state.
I am not anything.
I do not really exist.

ARC OF IDENTITY	1
CIRCLE OF ILLUSION	2
PATH OF THE CHILD	0
RITES OF PASSAGE	2
EXPRESSION	μ
PHYSIOMOTIONAL	-
COLOUR / SYMBOL	BLACK
KEYSTONES & MNEMONICS	SOMETHING IS MISSING
ELEMENT/IDIOM	FIRE/ELECTRICITY

III: OPPORTUNITY

When faced with opportunity, a "true sage" recognises that life holds up a mirror which shows the qualities needed to complete the journey. This is how we learn. Skills and abilities come from watching others. Wisdom comes from discipline and responsibility. Perhaps there is some aspect that is no longer of service? Be aware of the power of will, it leads to confident choices and mastery.

Everything needed for the journey is present. The trouble is, the possibility of awareness which gives rise to existence, goes unrecognised. The task is at hand, actualisation is at stake.

ARC OF IDENTITY	1
CIRCLE OF ILLUSION	2
PATH OF THE CHILD	0
RITES OF PASSAGE	3
EXPRESSION	ø
PHYSIOMOTIONAL	+
COLOUR / SYMBOL	MAGICIAN
KEYSTONES & MNEMONICS	Life reveals a problem
ELEMENT/IDIOM	FIRE/ELECTRICITY

THE SYSTEM

IV: INTUITION

Something is known that cannot be explained. It gives rise to the very question which becomes a driver for the madness. "Is something wrong?"

A "sage" looks beyond the answers found in books. Answers are at the edge of experience, not in the "knowledge about" experience. Unconscious mysteries provide the fertile ground in which creative events occur. Intuition is unrealised potential waiting for life force to bring it into expression.

While Opportunity (masculine) and Intuition (feminine) are equals, each is necessary for balance. It is time to turn away from the common sense world view and to look beyond the obvious by going deeper.

ARC OF IDENTITY	2
CIRCLE OF ILLUSION	3
PATH OF THE CHILD	0
RITES OF PASSAGE	4
EXPRESSION	ø
PHYSIOMOTIONAL	-
COLOUR / SYMBOL	HIGH PRIESTESS
KEYSTONES & MNEMONICS	It takes more than a sign
ELEMENT/IDIOM	FIRE/ELECTRICITY

V: FRIENDSHIP

Suddenly awareness refutes the common sense world view.
The survival of the "ego trick" comes under threat.
So what if wants are met only by first fulfilling needs?
Stability and security come under scrutiny.
The instinct is to fight or flee.
Despite the way things seem…
Fear is an ally that can help uncover the root of the problem.
This is human potential at ground zero.
A child learns character, to be personal.
An emotional state gets misidentified.
Seeking that state begins.

ARC OF IDENTITY	2
CIRCLE OF ILLUSION	3
PATH OF THE CHILD	1
RITES OF PASSAGE	5
EXPRESSION	¿
PHYSIOMOTIONAL	+
COLOUR / SYMBOL	SCARLET
KEYSTONES & MNEMONICS	MULADHARA
ELEMENT/IDIOM	FIRE/ELECTRICITY

THE SYSTEM

VI: ADVENTURE

Here and there are the same.
You have been down there.
You know the road.
You know exactly where it ends.
I am everything that is infinite.
I am only ever here.

ARC OF IDENTITY	2
CIRCLE OF ILLUSION	3
PATH OF THE CHILD	1
RITES OF PASSAGE	6
EXPRESSION	μ
PHYSIOMOTIONAL	-
COLOUR / SYMBOL	SCARLET
KEYSTONES & MNEMONICS	THE CALL
ELEMENT/IDIOM	FIRE/ELECTRICITY

VII: CREATIVITY

All physical acts carried out as expressions of visualisation are creative. Thoughts come in many forms, pictures, sensations and words. Creative thoughts are gut instincts. These are often directly conflicted by thoughts born out of the "knowledge about" things or internally voiced by languages.

Even the "I", "me", or "self" is a thought. Learn to switch from making thought wrong, to an appreciation of the natural cycle of things. Allow everything to nourish. A "true sage" recognises a compassionate mother can often be quite ruthless. Accept whatever happens without prejudice.

There are no right or wrong answers, some ideas simply outlive others. Recognition of the limitation of words, can lead to an experience of the abundance of life.

ARC OF IDENTITY	3
CIRCLE OF ILLUSION	4
PATH OF THE CHILD	1
RITES OF PASSAGE	7
EXPRESSION	ø
PHYSIOMOTIONAL	+
COLOUR / SYMBOL	EMPRESS
KEYSTONES & MNEMONICS	See you on the other side
ELEMENT/IDIOM	FIRE/ELECTRICITY

THE SYSTEM

VIII: RESPONSIBILITY

It is the response that says "it starts here, this is the cause". The illusion is all around, it is apparent everywhere we look. Responsibility gets felt at work, in rest, or at play. It gives rise to security, then provides direction. It is the basis of authority and a structure imposed upon chaos.

Certain behaviours are necessary for managing wellbeing. Life responds in predictable ways which can be explored through various disciplines. These restrictions can be frustrating, yet through patience the purpose can be understood.

A "sage" is born into a prison with an open gate and yet they cannot see a way out. As patterns emerge, a new kind of pleasure comes from discovering order.

Give up the role of victim!

Responsibility is a stern discipline which demands respect in leadership yet makes no other responsible. Think responsibly, see beyond the "ego trick" and stop blaming.

ARC OF IDENTITY	4
CIRCLE OF ILLUSION	4
PATH OF THE CHILD	1
RITES OF PASSAGE	8
EXPRESSION	ø
PHYSIOMOTIONAL	-
COLOUR / SYMBOL	EMPEROR
KEYSTONES & MNEMONICS	See you on the other side
ELEMENT/IDIOM	FIRE/ELECTRICITY

IX: INTELLECT

By all means learn the moral structure of society, develop, grow. Take heed of rules and intimately understand the delusion from within it. A "true sage" recognises they have been taken in by the greatest con life ever pulled... making us believe... that "knowledge about" is the truth.

Science is the new blind faith. The greatest enemy will hide in the last place you would ever look. Notice that righteous evangelists are the biggest threat.

Do not deny freedom exists until it is too late to do anything about it. Use everything you learn to break free from and subsequently unlearn whatever you think you already know.

ARC OF IDENTITY	5
CIRCLE OF ILLUSION	4
PATH OF THE CHILD	1
RITES OF PASSAGE	9
EXPRESSION	ø
PHYSIOMOTIONAL	+
COLOUR / SYMBOL	HIEROPHANT
KEYSTONES & MNEMONICS	See you on the other side
ELEMENT/IDIOM	FIRE/ELECTRICITY

THE SYSTEM

X: ACTION

What if you were unable to escape from the dream to save liberty?
Concepts are not real in the same way that objects are real.
There is no X, Y, or Z axis in reality.
I am everything that is multidimensional.
I am infinite depth.
Wake up.

ARC OF IDENTITY	5
CIRCLE OF ILLUSION	4
PATH OF THE CHILD	1
RITES OF PASSAGE	10
EXPRESSION	μ
PHYSIOMOTIONAL	-
COLOUR / SYMBOL	SCARLET
KEYSTONES & MNEMONICS	LOOKING GLASS
ELEMENT/IDIOM	FIRE/ELECTRICITY

Mark Ty-Wharton

XI: ALLIANCE

PILGRIMAGE
(First Threshold - Special World - The Seeker)

Humanity yearns for a deeper connection. Often this takes the form of a friendship, romance, or sexual union. A "true sage" recognises how easy and graceful life is when aptitude meets burning passion. However this is just the tip of the iceberg. There is only ever energy. Things change, happen and move. We think of energy as being love, yet love is simply energy.

The "ego trick" will create the illusion that you decide on your own beliefs. It will even make you believe that you are "true to yourself" when you are "doing what you love."

> *"Poets are known, artists are known to fall in love almost every day. Their love is like a rose flower. While it is there it is so fragrant, so alive, dancing in the wind, in the rain, in the sun, asserting its beauty. But by the evening it may be gone, and you cannot do anything to prevent it. The deeper love of the heart is just like a breeze that comes into your room, brings its freshness, coolness, and then it is gone. You cannot catch hold of the wind in your fist. Very few people are so courageous as to live with a moment-to-moment, changing life. Hence, they have decided to fall into a love on which they can depend."*
>
> OSHO

Finding help, only serves to illuminate problems and make them more apparent, amplifying the severity of the situation. A guru, mentor or teacher will often kick a dog when it is down. However, the problem doesn't get worse and the fact it becomes more apparent is ultimately a positive thing.

A preference for the positive is a worthy attribute where life is a celebration and not just merely survival. Attachment to positivity with a view that "this is the way it should always be" is a tyranny.

THE SYSTEM

Self-development is a reflection of imaginative ideas. Developing self in this way is in contradiction to that which is true. Self-expression is in direct opposition to the goal of actualisation.

Nobody becomes actualised.

The "ego trick" simply vanishes when it can be seen for what it really is. Know thy enemy. To hack a system it must be known intimately.

ARC OF IDENTITY	6
CIRCLE OF ILLUSION	5
PATH OF THE CHILD	1
RITES OF PASSAGE	11
EXPRESSION	ø
PHYSIOMOTIONAL	+
COLOUR / SYMBOL	LOVERS
KEYSTONES & MNEMONICS	The tip of the iceberg
ELEMENT/IDIOM	WOOD/MAGNETISM

Mark Ty-Wharton

XII: TIME

Time does not really exist in the way we think it does.
There is no fourth dimension.
Things change, happen and move.
Time is just a concept about absolute relationships.
With objects there are no absolutes.
I am everlasting momentum.

ARC OF IDENTITY	6
CIRCLE OF ILLUSION	5
PATH OF THE CHILD	1
RITES OF PASSAGE	12
EXPRESSION	μ
PHYSIOMOTIONAL	-
COLOUR / SYMBOL	SCARLET
KEYSTONES & MNEMONICS	EXISTENTIAL CRISIS
ELEMENT/IDIOM	WOOD/MAGNETISM

THE SYSTEM

XIII: CHOICE

The human potential movement is all about choice. Yet choice is only a symbol of forward motion in a world where everything already changes, happens and moves. Much of this kind of training creates the possibility of free will and encourages active pursuit of life's goals. Assertion, empowerment and taking charge. Inner control, triumph over environment.

Mastery over the self through hard work and determination will carry life quickly forward and single minded focus is often a step in the direction of actualisation. Unfortunately, the "ego trick" fools us into thinking we have achieved something.

A "true sage" recognises that choosing to make affirmations can only provide short lived benefit and eventually amplifies and illuminates the severity of the problem of apparent separation.

This "false entity" is an illusion, yet certain actions, causes, effects and outcomes need to occur for the extent of the illusion to be seen. The "I", "me", or "self" is a paradox. Single minded zeal is required for mastery of the mind and yet the mind has no true master.

Drive, focus on success, teaching yourself that you can count on yourself and others, will eventually lead to the collapse of identification with a central force that is responsible for the single minded focus.

ARC OF IDENTITY	7
CIRCLE OF ILLUSION	5
PATH OF THE CHILD	1
RITES OF PASSAGE	13
EXPRESSION	ø
PHYSIOMOTIONAL	+
COLOUR / SYMBOL	CHARIOT
KEYSTONES & MNEMONICS	The tip of the iceberg
ELEMENT/IDIOM	WOOD/MAGNETISM

XIV: GENEROSITY

Money is not real, it has no fixed value and is not a measure of worth.
True generosity gives without prejudice or expectation.
Focus attention enthusiastically, this is true generosity.
Avoid "tit for tat" relationships. Walk away from righteousness.
The "ego trick" is a prison for the mind which cannot be seen.
Be in the story to notice the story and set thought free.
Give up addiction to basic emotional needs.
A mind that is free to think meets every emotional need.
Obstacles can be overwhelmingly strong.
Yet, don't let joy become a curse.
Pleasure can lead to violence .
Seek positives outcomes generously.

ARC OF IDENTITY	7
CIRCLE OF ILLUSION	5
PATH OF THE CHILD	2
RITES OF PASSAGE	14
EXPRESSION	¿
PHYSIOMOTIONAL	-
COLOUR / SYMBOL	AMBER
KEYSTONES & MNEMONICS	SWADHISTHANA
ELEMENT/IDIOM	WOOD/MAGNETISM

XV: CHARACTER

Life presents new challenges. Develop strength of character and inner resolve. A "true sage" recognises the character as an "ego trick" or pattern, which was simply born out of the language of a mechanistic consciousness.

See beyond the boundaries, constraints and limitations of the terminological overlay that knowledge imposes on reality. The character played in the story gets noticed. This is the first step to understanding there is no "false entity" of a separate "I", "me", or "self." This illusion is an integral part of conditioning; the unique patterns which distinguish each of us from other.

At times passions surface which can be realised through a softer approach. Understanding the need for patience and acceptance in some things. A balanced sense of compassion, fairness and forgiveness give courage and endurance in difficult times.

ARC OF IDENTITY	8
CIRCLE OF ILLUSION	6
PATH OF THE CHILD	2
RITES OF PASSAGE	15
EXPRESSION	ø
PHYSIOMOTIONAL	+
COLOUR / SYMBOL	STRENGTH
KEYSTONES & MNEMONICS	Unexpected aspects
ELEMENT/IDIOM	WOOD/MAGNETISM

XVI: MEANING

The mind does not work like a computer.
The mind stores meaning not events or information.
I am the meaning I give to life.
I am the story.

ARC OF IDENTITY	8
CIRCLE OF ILLUSION	6
PATH OF THE CHILD	2
RITES OF PASSAGE	16
EXPRESSION	μ
PHYSIOMOTIONAL	-
COLOUR / SYMBOL	AMBER
KEYSTONES & MNEMONICS	UNEXPECTED EVENTS
ELEMENT/IDIOM	WOOD/MAGNETISM

THE SYSTEM

XVII: REFLECTION

Know thy enemy. Contemplation can lead to understanding. Introspection should always seek to answer exogenically. When any given system is understood from within, its limitations can be usurped and overcome. A "true sage" recognises consciousness - the ultimate continuous evolutionary upgrade - the pattern of thought that identifies you, yet adapts and grows to hide the truth.

Reality consists of momentum in progress. Any event stream or process can influence any other. Outcomes are given by the morphological influence of one event over another.

Each event shapes every other and each are in relative relationships. Expected outcomes can influence current affairs and pull for those tangible realities to come into being as readily as memories can influence actions and the course of events.

Deeper truths are realised, and world views change, when withdrawing and alone in reflection and meditation.

It is wise to ask "Which way is up?" and "Why?"

ARC OF IDENTITY	9
CIRCLE OF ILLUSION	6
PATH OF THE CHILD	2
RITES OF PASSAGE	17
EXPRESSION	ø
PHYSIOMOTIONAL	+
COLOUR / SYMBOL	HERMIT
KEYSTONES & MNEMONICS	Unexpected aspects
ELEMENT/IDIOM	WOOD/MAGNETISM

XVIII: POWER

Notice when we let go of dreams, they can manifest spontaneously.
Notice personal opinions are complex ideas formed by the "ego trick".
Let go of anxiety, fear and introversion.
These give rise to depression, which does not serve life.
Expand and grow into what you really are.
True power serves all.

ARC OF IDENTITY	9
CIRCLE OF ILLUSION	6
PATH OF THE CHILD	3
RITES OF PASSAGE	18
EXPRESSION	¿
PHYSIOMOTIONAL	-
COLOUR / SYMBOL	SAFFRON
KEYSTONES & MNEMONICS	MANIPURA
ELEMENT/IDIOM	WOOD/MAGNETISM

THE SYSTEM

XIX: CHAOS

Q. Is there free will, or is everything predetermined?
A. Neither is true

A "true sage" recognises that this is the wrong question and starts to see how things connect. The game of the "ego trick" is to fool us into thinking that as long as there is no predetermined future, then there has to be free will. To an extent, our choices over the context of past actions predetermine aspects of the future. Yet free will suffers at the mercy of cause and effect.

What happens next, will be what happens next. Mechanistic science tries to treat change cinematographically, as if there are a series of static moments in a paradigm called past, present and future. Then, now and soon. Before, THIS and after. THIS is the perpetual nowless wonder of nowlessness.

There is no moment in momentum.

Everything is always in flux.

> *"We are in the position of a little child entering a huge library filled with books in many different languages. The child knows someone must have written those books. It does not know how. It does not understand the languages in which they are written. The child dimly suspects a mysterious order in the arrangement of the books but doesn't know what it is. That, it seems to me, is the attitude of even the most intelligent human being toward God. We see a universe marvelously arranges and obeying certain laws, but only dimly understand these laws. Our limited minds cannot grasp the mysterious force that moves the constellations."*
>
> Albert Einstein

The solution is to notice imagination is the wondrous tool that gives rise to everything and yet, in and of itself, it does not really exist. Imagination is the subjective and it is not an object. There are no rules and yet liberty is at stake and at the heart of the matter is always the rules. Wheresoever you may wander, the villain is always at hand. Tricking us into thinking that the thoughts are us. That the narrative of thought is who we are.

ARC OF IDENTITY	10
CIRCLE OF ILLUSION	7
PATH OF THE CHILD	3
RITES OF PASSAGE	19
EXPRESSION	ø
PHYSIOMOTIONAL	+
COLOUR / SYMBOL	WHEEL
KEYSTONES & MNEMONICS	A life or death situation
ELEMENT/IDIOM	WOOD/MAGNETISM

THE SYSTEM

XX: TRUTH

Where is the "I", "me", or "self" located?
Devotion, equilibrium, unconditional acceptance.
Love soars in the chest from the belly to the heart.
Take flight and leave this conceptual prison.
Thought is not inside the head looking out.
And spirit is not inside the body.
Compassion, tenderness.
Let it fly between lives.
Radiate clear light.
Ease and grace.

ARC OF IDENTITY	10
CIRCLE OF ILLUSION	7
PATH OF THE CHILD	4
RITES OF PASSAGE	20
EXPRESSION	¿
PHYSIOMOTIONAL	-
COLOUR / SYMBOL	EMERALD
KEYSTONES & MNEMONICS	ANAHATA
ELEMENT/IDIOM	WOOD/MAGNETISM

XXI: FAIRNESS

Responsibility is simply a declaration that can be made about life's causes and effects. It does not right wrongs, it simply states "it starts here." A "true sage" recognises that the traffic of thought (both conscious and unconscious) dictates the perceived reality of life. To be a grand architect there needs to be fairness, honesty and justice. Going against the flow and asking "what's in it for me?" will only ever imprison the "ego trick" in a false sense of pride and thus hide the key to liberty.

The way things are perceived can alter beliefs, choices and outcomes. Brutal honesty is often more affective at wiping the slate clean, than the wheel of karma. It is wise to settle old debts.

All is not fair in love and war.

Deceiving others to get what you want is ultimately self-defeating. Being the cause in the matter of life starts with a declaration of separation and ultimately ends with a recognition of unity. Recognition that we are all one is a moral turning point in the journey.

Take responsibility for past actions.

Fight separation with unity

Remain true to insights.

ARC OF IDENTITY	11
CIRCLE OF ILLUSION	7
PATH OF THE CHILD	4
RITES OF PASSAGE	21
EXPRESSION	ø
PHYSIOMOTIONAL	+
COLOUR / SYMBOL	JUSTICE
KEYSTONES & MNEMONICS	A life or death situation
ELEMENT/IDIOM	WOOD/MAGNETISM

THE SYSTEM

XXII: CONTEXT

There is only ever what is happening.
I fight to create stability in my relationship with life.
Yet the stability I create is the only reality.
The context is only true by definition.
It is the background of relatedness.
I come from this place.

ARC OF IDENTITY	11
CIRCLE OF ILLUSION	7
PATH OF THE CHILD	4
RITES OF PASSAGE	22
EXPRESSION	μ
PHYSIOMOTIONAL	-
COLOUR / SYMBOL	EMERALD
KEYSTONES & MNEMONICS	IT ALL TURNS TO DUST
ELEMENT/IDIOM	WOOD/MAGNETISM

XXIII: FAITH

REVOLUTION
(Second Threshold - Battle - The Crusader)

When life is humbling, let go. It is wise to rethink choices and notice that, when the struggle for control is relinquished, surprising things can happen. Personal defeat can become universal triumph. All is not lost. Control is part of the illusion, in reality, life itself is a function of chaos.

Surrender, it is time to stop trying to manifest a different reality and to learn the truth about this current reality you believe yourself to be in. Put aside self interest in favour of unity and any work which sets out to achieve a higher purpose. A "true sage" recognises how to suspend action and to wait for opportunities which can create new paths to follow.

This is movement at rest. In Taoism, Wu Wei, non-action or non-doing. Free of urgency or pressure. Surrender to flow, then trust in the process of life and engage in its spontaneous effortless movement. By behaving in a completely natural, uncontrived way it becomes possible to discover the miraculous support of effortless, timeless, acceptance.

ARC OF IDENTITY	12
CIRCLE OF ILLUSION	8
PATH OF THE CHILD	4
RITES OF PASSAGE	23
EXPRESSION	ø
PHYSIOMOTIONAL	+
COLOUR / SYMBOL	HANGED MAN
KEYSTONES & MNEMONICS	Use everything for growth
ELEMENT/IDIOM	ICE/WATER/STEAM

THE SYSTEM

XXIV: GROWTH

Use everything that happens as a catalyst to grow.

ARC OF IDENTITY	12
CIRCLE OF ILLUSION	8
PATH OF THE CHILD	4
RITES OF PASSAGE	24
EXPRESSION	μ
PHYSIOMOTIONAL	-
COLOUR / SYMBOL	EMERALD
KEYSTONES & MNEMONICS	DO WHAT THOU WILT
ELEMENT/IDIOM	ICE/WATER/STEAM

Mark Ty-Wharton

XXV: CHANGES

This is a time of changes, transitioning into a new chapter. The old ways are over, no longer of service. Focusing only on essentials is inevitable and unavoidable. A "true sage" recognises that changes are self-evident. Growth, then decay is inherent in all things.

There is existence. For existence to be recognised there must be sentience. Whenever one thing relies on another thing, there is duality. Duality always shows up within a single paradigm.

This paradigm is a combination of coexisting factors which in turn create pure unity. Where seemingly opposite ideas gel into a single coherent context that gives rise to those ideas. In the paradigm of awareness, or experience, given by existence and sentience, what becomes apparent is that we live in a mechanistic universe where material objects change, happen and move.

Changes happen and move with duration and relative to one another, yet all within the cohesive whole. Changes provide a clear pointer for those who seek an answer to the mystery of "I Am". The familiar "ego trick" vanishes and gives rise to a point of view which can give a different quality to life once it is seen.

ARC OF IDENTITY	13
CIRCLE OF ILLUSION	8
PATH OF THE CHILD	4
RITES OF PASSAGE	25
EXPRESSION	ø
PHYSIOMOTIONAL	+
COLOUR / SYMBOL	DEATH
KEYSTONES & MNEMONICS	Use everything for growth
ELEMENT/IDIOM	ICE/WATER/STEAM

THE SYSTEM

XXVI: LAUGHTER

Laughter is the lucid dreamer expressing growth.
Thoughts are fluent.
Independence.
Security.

ARC OF IDENTITY	13
CIRCLE OF ILLUSION	8
PATH OF THE CHILD	5
RITES OF PASSAGE	26
EXPRESSION	¿
PHYSIOMOTIONAL	-
COLOUR / SYMBOL	COBALT
KEYSTONES & MNEMONICS	VISHUDDHA
ELEMENT/IDIOM	ICE/WATER/STEAM

XXVII: BALANCE

Yin cannot exist without Yang. Each and every action has an equal and opposite counter action. Every concept has an opposing view point which allows for its very existence. Every state has a balancing state. Each mood is a paradigm. Happiness opposes sadness. Love opposes hate.

A "true sage" recognises (even while swinging wildly back and forth on an emotional pendulum) it can be noticed that polar opposites give rise to a spectrum of stillness. At the very heart of momentum there is balance.

Newton's third law of motion states: When one body exerts a force on a second body, the second body simultaneously exerts a force equal in magnitude and opposite in direction on the first body.

It is in this paradox that life ceases to occur as an either/or phenomena and there can be an approach to emotional equilibrium.

The "ego trick" fades into the dark night of the soul. In this existential crisis, something is seen which can illuminate life in such a way that, identity can be present without causing daily frustrations to rise to the level of unnecessary suffering.

ARC OF IDENTITY	14
CIRCLE OF ILLUSION	9
PATH OF THE CHILD	5
RITES OF PASSAGE	27
EXPRESSION	ø
PHYSIOMOTIONAL	+
COLOUR / SYMBOL	TEMPERANCE
KEYSTONES & MNEMONICS	The dark night
ELEMENT/IDIOM	ICE/WATER/STEAM

THE SYSTEM

XXVIII: SOUL

There is no individual soul.
I am universal life force energy.
My true nature is THE nature.
I am universal spirit.

ARC OF IDENTITY	14
CIRCLE OF ILLUSION	9
PATH OF THE CHILD	5
RITES OF PASSAGE	28
EXPRESSION	µ
PHYSIOMOTIONAL	-
COLOUR / SYMBOL	COBALT
KEYSTONES & MNEMONICS	THE DARK NIGHT
ELEMENT/IDIOM	ICE/WATER/STEAM

XXIX: TEARS

A recognition that catalysts need to be present for changes to occur.
Tears express disruption and release.
Tears calm anger and pain.
Signals an end to duality.
Intuitive OM.
Expansion.

ARC OF IDENTITY	14
CIRCLE OF ILLUSION	9
PATH OF THE CHILD	6
RITES OF PASSAGE	29
EXPRESSION	¿
PHYSIOMOTIONAL	+
COLOUR / SYMBOL	INDIGO
KEYSTONES & MNEMONICS	AJNA
ELEMENT/IDIOM	ICE/WATER/STEAM

THE SYSTEM

XXX: SHADOW

Darkness is not a sinister phenomenon without the existence of light. For every light source there is a shadow. It represents form, yet has the ability to change perspective, shape shift, silhouette or represent itself as larger than life. Shadows are like ghosts, or demons. Demons yearn form, believing their hosts to have a spirit or soul. A "sage" who sells his soul to a demon, ghost or shadow learns that the soul is not an object which can be possessed. It is an illusion that there is any substance to the "false entity" of the "ego trick."

The shadow is present, visible yet can never be captured because like a reflection in a looking glass, it has no tangible reality.

> *"A satisfactory theory of the universe has to be one that's worth betting on. It seems to me absolutely elementary common sense. If you make a theory of the universe which isn't worth betting on, why bother, just commit suicide. But if you want to go on playing the game you've got to have an optimal theory for playing the game. Otherwise there is no point in it."*
>
> Alan Watts

In classical Roman religion, the individual instance of a general divine nature that is present in every individual person, place, or thing is called the genius. Mythological sites throughout the Western Roman Empire dedicate altars to a particular genius loci, or the protective spirit of a place.

The energy of genius arises from outside everything you believe yourself to be. Freedom occurs when one has sold their soul to a devil only to realise they never had an individual soul. As for the devil, her habit of engaging in contracts for souls only serves to further the illusion of her own separation, by believing she has control over another soul. She is so trapped by the "ego trick" that her addiction to power blinds her from "innate truth."

When the "ego trick" gains favour and becomes a control mechanism, the darkness has won. When potential is freed and "innate truth" is realised, light illuminates without shadows. Then it can be seen that energy, life force, spirit and soul are collective. That between the devil and the deep blue sea, every rock star who ever sold their soul was ultimately set free.

ARC OF IDENTITY	15
CIRCLE OF ILLUSION	9
PATH OF THE CHILD	6
RITES OF PASSAGE	30
EXPRESSION	ø
PHYSIOMOTIONAL	-
COLOUR / SYMBOL	DEVIL
KEYSTONES & MNEMONICS	The dark night
ELEMENT/IDIOM	ICE/WATER/STEAM

THE SYSTEM

XXXI: METAMORPHOSIS

True liberation is a recognition that there never was anyone to liberate.
There was only ever an anthropomorphic God.
The "ego trick" had no real character.
Nothing really dies except hope.
I am the realisation of new hope.
I have what I need to fight.
I am actualised.

ARC OF IDENTITY	16
CIRCLE OF ILLUSION	10
PATH OF THE CHILD	6
RITES OF PASSAGE	31
EXPRESSION	μ
PHYSIOMOTIONAL	+
COLOUR / SYMBOL	INDIGO
KEYSTONES & MNEMONICS	RESSURECTION
ELEMENT/IDIOM	ICE/WATER/STEAM

XXXII: RETREAT

Cathartic rebellion purges everything. The worst that can happen is that we identify with the "ego trick" and use it to protect and control. While it seems we have provided a fortress for this "I", "me", or "self", the mental construct imprisons us from "innate truth". And so there becomes a total withdrawal from life.

When life is overwhelming, anxiety can arise in the body and cause a fight, flight, or freeze response. The revelation comes when it can be noticed that there is nothing negative in this response. Life is breathing in as well as breathing out. People who have lost everything in a natural disaster quickly learn they retain the one thing which is most valuable. A "sage" makes necessary adjustments during such a crisis.

When it can be seen that destruction and instability always follow a long period of growth, it becomes easier to accept that a natural consequence of such situations is to create the conditions for rebirth.

When there is no real reason to face life head on, sometimes it is better to retreat. Unpredictable and chaotic change is the nature of life. All of the crises, upheaval and humbling blows, all of the anger and disruption were simply catalysts for that which needed to occur next.

ARC OF IDENTITY	16
CIRCLE OF ILLUSION	10
PATH OF THE CHILD	6
RITES OF PASSAGE	32
EXPRESSION	ø
PHYSIOMOTIONAL	-
COLOUR / SYMBOL	TOWER
KEYSTONES & MNEMONICS	Rising from the ashes
ELEMENT/IDIOM	ICE/WATER/STEAM

XXXIII: REBIRTH

At last a symbol of healing, hope and rejuvenation. Fortunes are changing. Faith is restored. When the heart is open, love pours out freely.

The truth about life is no longer hidden behind the story of life.

A "true sage" recognises that when peace comes after a storm, the belly of the whale might actually have provided protection. Calmness, serenity. Now is the time to face life and make necessary changes.

A radiant star in a cloudless sky gives energy to all life, a beacon of hope and inspiration. A revelation is experienced, "innate truth" is actualised. Life is filled with joy and wishes to share generosity with the world. This in turn creates confidence and trust. Be aware of life's blessings.

In striving for higher meaning and existence, love flows, nothing is held back and there is a recognition of the difference between self-realisation and truth actualisation.

ARC OF IDENTITY	17
CIRCLE OF ILLUSION	10
PATH OF THE CHILD	6
RITES OF PASSAGE	33
EXPRESSION	ø
PHYSIOMOTIONAL	+
COLOUR / SYMBOL	STAR
KEYSTONES & MNEMONICS	Rising from the ashes
ELEMENT/IDIOM	ICE/WATER/STEAM

Mark Ty-Wharton

XXXIV: IMAGINATION

Enlightenment perpetuates the illusion if it is seen as enlightenment. There can even be an experience of abiding bliss. Yet, bliss is a vulnerability. Sooner or later something will challenge this perfect calm. Joy is a feeling state not an "innate truth" and while positive emotions may arise in meditation if they are not yet subject to mental clarity they will pass like clouds across the moon.

Imagination can make us susceptible to fantasy, distortion and a false picture of the truth. Go further!

> *"Binker-what I call him-is a secret of my own,*
> *And Binker is the reason why I never feel alone.*
> *Playing in the nursery, sitting on the stair,*
> *Whatever I am busy at, Binker will be there.*
> *Binker's always talking, 'cos I'm teaching him to speak;*
> *He sometimes likes to do it in a funny sort of squeak,*
> *And he sometimes like to do it in a hoodling sort of roar.*
> *And I have to do it for him 'cos his throat is rather sore.*
> *Binker's brave as lions when we're running in the park;*
> *Binker's brave as tigers when we're lying in the dark;*
> *Binker's brave as elephants. He never, never cries..*
> *Except (like other people) when the soap gets in his eyes.*
> *Binker isn't greedy, but he does like things to eat,*
> *So I have to say to people when they're giving me a sweet,*
> *Oh, Binker wants a chocolate, so could you give me two?*
> *And then I eat it for him, 'cos his teeth are rather new."*
> A.A.Milne, Now We Are Six

What sets humanity aside from other species is the degree to which we use imagination. When imagination can be stimulated in positive ways, what gets seen can be used for growth and new doors start to open.

THE SYSTEM

Imagination can be the seat of anxiety, fear and limiting belief systems, yet it can also be used to transform those same fears and anxieties, unrealistic expectations and false ideals. When it can be seen that imagination gives rise to the story itself, that the story is separate to reality, then these unwanted side effects, such as confusion, deception and lack of clarity can be resolved.

The Cogito ergo sum doesn't quite add up. Thinking about existence, only proves existence. Who we think we really are is only ever imagined. In logic perhaps a statement of truth must occur, like this: "whatever has the property of thinking, must exist." This cannot be subject to any method of doubt, because it appears as self-evident. Descartes should probably have just said "thinking is happening." But when you think about it, in reality, where does thinking exist? The Cartesian world view assumes the existence of a thinking thing, yet the reference to "I", "me", or "self" is a claim that cogito can't justify.

It is an "innate truth" to recognise thought exists directly in experience yet has no discernible fixed location. We think, therefore we think we are and there is only existence. Imagination is an aspect of this existence. It can show up as a thought and it can visualise duality, yet it still occurs within unity.

We imagine ourselves into a separate existence as a soul in charge of a bio-mechanism, yet like the moon, we have no separate light source. Any light we carry is merely a reflection of the light of the source of all energy in this place. A sage who asks "what is the source of existence?" will come closer to understanding reality than a sage who mistakenly asserts "I am."

ARC OF IDENTITY	18
CIRCLE OF ILLUSION	10
PATH OF THE CHILD	6
RITES OF PASSAGE	34
EXPRESSION	Ø
PHYSIOMOTIONAL	-
COLOUR / SYMBOL	MOON
KEYSTONES & MNEMONICS	Rising from the ashes
ELEMENT/IDIOM	ICE/WATER/STEAM

XXXV: HOPE

ACTUALISATION
(Third Threshold - Suffering - The Return)

Optimism for the human race. A "true sage" recognises universal hope comes from a willingness to give up everything they imagined themselves to be, for liberty. By gaining insight and understanding, it appears that for the first time there is true freedom, filled with rising joy and enthusiasm.

An inner light shines into hidden places, dispels the clouds of confusion and fear and illuminates this whole being.

No challenge is too daunting.

Substantial victory.

ARC OF IDENTITY	19
CIRCLE OF ILLUSION	11
PATH OF THE CHILD	6
RITES OF PASSAGE	35
EXPRESSION	ø
PHYSIOMOTIONAL	VICTORY
COLOUR / SYMBOL	SUN
KEYSTONES & MNEMONICS	Must be willing to give up
ELEMENT/IDIOM	WIND/COOL BREEZE

THE SYSTEM

XXXVI: ANGER

How can anger be an expression of actualisation?
Why are these emotions beyond control?
What happened to calm intellect?
Where is my compassion?
Surely this is wrong?

ARC OF IDENTITY	19
CIRCLE OF ILLUSION	11
PATH OF THE CHILD	6
RITES OF PASSAGE	36
EXPRESSION	μ
PHYSIOMOTIONAL	SETBACK
COLOUR / SYMBOL	CLEAR
KEYSTONES & MNEMONICS	WORST THAT CAN HAPPEN
ELEMENT/IDIOM	WIND/COOL BREEZE

Mark Ty-Wharton

XXXVII: APPROVAL

All seems lost. Disaster. Failure. The situation seems hopeless. There is nothing to be gained from an expression of personal power. It is only ever vanity to suggest your own becoming to others. In the presence of actualisation, actions speak louder than words. And yet it is close. Only through a willingness to give up everything, can the journey pass the gateway without a gate to the promise of actualisation.

In the story of Canute the great vs. the waves, it can clearly be seen that control cannot be exercised over the supreme power of the elements. True personal power is the expression of absolution through forgiveness and humility. The tide cannot be turned back unless rebirth, through dissolution of "false entity", causes the "ego trick" to vanish.

"There is something about yourself that you don't know. Something that you will deny even exists until it's too late to do anything about it. It's the only reason you get up in the morning, the only reason you suffer the shifty boss, the blood, the sweat and the tears. This is because you want people to know how good, attractive, generous, funny, wild and clever you really are. 'Fear or revere me, but please think I'm special.' We share an addiction. We're approval junkies. We're all in it for the slap on the back and the gold watch. The 'hip, hip, who-funky-rah.' Look at the clever boy with the badge, polishing his trophy. Shine on, you crazy diamond. Cos we're just monkeys wrapped in suits, begging for the approval of others."
Jake Green, Revolver (2005)

The situation is hopeless without humility. Rise up to fulfil the promise of actualisation and give up the addiction to approval. Only when the "ego trick" is vanished can doubts and hesitations be relinquished. A day of reckoning is at hand, yet any attempt to sanction the actions of others must also be a recognition that such an approval is always a judgement. A "sage" who seeks approval, will

THE SYSTEM

only create hopelessness, which in turn becomes a sure fire way to perpetuate fear. The most fundamental fear is that the pretence of "false entity" will be seen through. The radiance of a transformation into a new state of being becomes possible through shedding "false entity."

What appears to be a personal day of reckoning is more accurately the birth of an impersonal role. Joy is at life's centre and this is realised by expressing joy as "innate truth" such that YOU ARE the experience of joy itself and not a being that experiences joy.

ARC OF IDENTITY	20
CIRCLE OF ILLUSION	11
PATH OF THE CHILD	6
RITES OF PASSAGE	37
EXPRESSION	ø
PHYSIOMOTIONAL	BIG NO
COLOUR / SYMBOL	JUDGEMENT
KEYSTONES & MNEMONICS	Must be willing to give up
ELEMENT/IDIOM	WIND/COOL BREEZE

XXXVIII: PEACE

Enlightenment is not an upgrade. A "sage" who thinks they became enlightened, came unprepared, boasts only vanity and wears the crown of false pride. The story of enlightenment has never been a story of becoming. Actualisation is the recognition that things are the way things always were.

Actualisation is not a permanent state, it happens in momentum. Samadhi has no fixed property or value. It is neither subject, nor object. The mind cannot truly find peace in a pure state of consciousness until this has been seen.

ARC OF IDENTITY	21
CIRCLE OF ILLUSION	12
PATH OF THE CHILD	7
RITES OF PASSAGE	38
EXPRESSION	¿
PHYSIOMOTIONAL	~
COLOUR / SYMBOL	CLEAR
KEYSTONES & MNEMONICS	SAHASARA
ELEMENT/IDIOM	WIND/COOL BREEZE

THE SYSTEM

XXXIX: FREEDOM

The "I", "me", or "self" of the "ego trick" is at peace.
Unique patterns distinguish apparent separation.
I am awareness and experience.
This is Elysium.
The stillness.
I am light.
I trust.

ARC OF IDENTITY	21
CIRCLE OF ILLUSION	12
PATH OF THE CHILD	7
RITES OF PASSAGE	39
EXPRESSION	µ
PHYSIOMOTIONAL	~
COLOUR / SYMBOL	CLEAR
KEYSTONES & MNEMONICS	FINAL BATTLE
ELEMENT/IDIOM	WIND/COOL BREEZE

XXXX: SUCCESS

Wholeness and complete understanding. A "true sage" recognises all matter is sentience. Intelligence is the function of the complexity of the neural network of any given matter. The size and scale of the universe makes this planet seem unimaginably small and fleeting. Yet everything flourishes and prospers, expressing the gift of life, through examination of momentum in nothing. Savour stillness.

By taking stillness as a point of view it is possible to have an experience that all of life changes within this stillness. The experience is full and meaningful.

The goal has been attained, recognised. Needs can be met over wants. The lessons of a journey are shared in preparation for subsequent journeys.

Remember that SUCCESS is only ever an illusion. The tree of life has no real beginning and is ultimately everlasting. Zero and infinity are the same.

Nothing is separate as a "true sage", a "true sage" as thought, a "true sage" as senses, a "true sage" as reality.

Suffering ends.

ARC OF IDENTITY	21
CIRCLE OF ILLUSION	12
PATH OF THE CHILD	7
RITES OF PASSAGE	40
EXPRESSION	ø
PHYSIOMOTIONAL	~
COLOUR / SYMBOL	WORLD
KEYSTONES & MNEMONICS	Master of two worlds
ELEMENT/IDIOM	WIND/COOL BREEZE

THE SYSTEM

Notes

Card face images appear courtesy of individual creator/owner(s) under the Creative Commons version 2.0 Attribution licence. It is not possible to add the licence details to each individual card. Instead, a full list of credits appear here in this (e)book which is an integral part of this complete work 'The System' and which should always accompany the cards and the audio book.

None of these images are derivative works, though due to the nature of the layout and printing process, some may have been cropped slightly, or may not appear in their entirety. Images are credited beneath each card name and a link is provided to the original image.

While you are free to share the image portion of the card under its original licence, 'The System' itself is published under a separate licence and you may not copy or distribute images of the cards in any form, for any purpose, without prior permission.

POTENTIAL
Child Tending Broken Baby Seedling by D. Sharon Pruitt
https://flic.kr/p/68QFDp

IDENTITY
Identity and Ration Books by Herry Lawford
https://flic.kr/p/64vP9z

OPPORTUNITY
Touch Healthy Soil by Natural Resources Conservation Service Soil Health Campaign
https://flic.kr/p/dgEUTf

INTUITION
Waiting by Angela Marie Henriette
https://flic.kr/p/aecmuK

FRIENDSHIP
Fly with me by Alice Popkorn
https://flic.kr/p/51hMDM

ADVENTURE
Adventures by Janet Ramsden
https://flic.kr/p/f543LJ

CREATIVITY
Creative by Victor1558
https://flic.kr/p/bpss6D

RESPONSIBILITY
Let Me Tell You Something Son by Reddy Aprianto
https://flic.kr/p/foubks

Mark Ty-Wharton

INTELLECT
Sharing Silent Moments by Chrismatos
https://flic.kr/p/aSQqek

ACTION
Well, finally! by Reinis Traidas
https://flic.kr/p/Be17E

ALLIANCE
Song of Rose by Angela Marie Henriette
https://flic.kr/p/5RvHi8

TIME
Travelling through Time and diving into my Universe... by Cyril Rana
https://flic.kr/p/cMgbim

CHOICE
Choice by William Ward
https://flic.kr/p/aQnVH4

GENEROSITY
Showers Of Love by D. Sharon Pruitt
https://flic.kr/p/k1l5po

CHARACTER
Janus Masks by Nathan Jones
https://flic.kr/p/U5bWu

MEANING
Uneven Means by K J Payne
https://flic.kr/p/8hFDmx

REFLECTION
Buddhism by Roberto Trm
https://flic.kr/p/bWLNxu

POWER
Arrive by Alice Popkorn
https://flic.kr/p/5uE9oP

CHAOS
Roulette Elevator by Brian Cantoni
https://flic.kr/p/fPvDam

TRUTH
0226 by CIA DE FOTO
https://flic.kr/p/5MzaGU

FAIRNESS
Old Scale by Alex
https://flic.kr/p/6hcfiQ

CONTEXT
Cross Section of a Tree's Roots by Aaron Escobar
https://flic.kr/p/4V2gr9

THE SYSTEM

FAITH
Trust by Vagawi
https://flic.kr/p/5NQfz1

GROWTH
Opportunity Is Missed by Sergei Tereschenko
https://flic.kr/p/eiSbHh

CHANGES
Day Of The Dead 6 by David Sorich
https://flic.kr/p/dq9aBa

LAUGHTER
0216 by CIA DE FOTO
https://flic.kr/p/5AR9gd

BALANCE
Red grape by Tomas Sobek
https://flic.kr/p/7p84hw

SOUL
Spirit by 29cm
https://flic.kr/p/c7xe9

TEARS
Crying child by Binu Kumar
https://flic.kr/p/6VGRhr

SHADOW
Satan's Little Helper by Paul Walker
https://flic.kr/p/6K5RvN

METAMORPHOSIS
Chrysalis to Butterfly (#1 of 5) by Sid Mosdell
https://flic.kr/p/bGSuax

RETREAT
New York / World Trade Centre by hom26
https://flic.kr/p/fmwefk

REBIRTH
God's Blessing by Jose Roberto V Moraes
https://flic.kr/p/6AeUBj

IMAGINATION
October 25th Cloudy Moonlight by Audrey
https://flic.kr/p/3GcAZ9

HOPE
Carpe Diem by Chad Cooper
https://flic.kr/p/fhDfsy

ANGER
Smashing Waves by Monika Thorpe
https://flic.kr/p/8Gb2Z9

Mark Ty-Wharton

APPROVAL
Scrolls by Clarence
https://flic.kr/p/7qxPk3

PEACE
Faith by Stefano Mortellaro
https://flic.kr/p/2ZCjS

FREEDOM
Tame Birds Sing About Freedom. Wild Birds Fly by Nico Kaiser
https://flic.kr/p/aqCMsD

SUCCESS
Eye by Mario
https://flic.kr/p/e3CA4

THE SYSTEM

Made in the USA
Monee, IL
03 May 2026

49437960R00044